a poetry collection

*for the younger
heart in me.*

Published by LB Publishing, LLC

Original edition ISBN: 979-8-9918718-3-9

A Poetry Collection – For the younger heart in me. Copyright © 2025 by Lanna Brasure

All rights reserved.

The author and the publisher assume no responsibility for any injuries suffered or damages or losses as a result of reading this book.

No part of this publication may be reproduced, distributed, or transmitted in any form or by any means, including photocopying, recording, or other electronic or mechanical methods, without the prior written permission of the publisher or author. For permission requests, contact LB Publishing, LLC at hello@lb-publishing.com.

*A collection of poetry
written by Lanna Brasure*

Dedicated to the younger version of myself who wrote these words and felt the emotions to produce them.

I believe in you.

And even if nobody else likes them….they are released now.

I wrote some of these poems over 20 years ago.

Some of them I no longer agree with.

Some of them I think are terrible.

But some of them still make me feel things when I read them.

I can feel the exact emotions I felt at the exact moment I was constructing these pieces of art.

Whether we admire our own work or not does not always matter, for we can always help others with the things we don't love most about ourselves and our work.

I release these into the world to hopefully help others with pain, loss, loneliness, and their own sense of personal torture.

These words are art.

Capturing moments, experiences, and emotions in time.

We all long to connect and resonate with others.

And, to feel something.

I release these words into the world in hopes of that – that you feel something.

boop.

I don't believe in love yet because I'm just too young.

I don't believe in love yet because my dating has just begun.

I don't believe in love yet because I just don't want to.

I don't believe in love yet because it's just too much to go through.

I don't believe in love yet although it must be a wonderful feeling.

I don't believe in love yet because of what I'm fearing.

I don't believe in love yet because it could all go down the drain.

I don't believe in love yet because of all the pain.

I don't believe in love yet because it takes a lot of trust,

It takes a lot of work, and love could just be lust.

I wish you had my eyes,

To see this confident mess,

Standing right before me,

I have one goal before I rest.

For you to see your beauty,

The way I have seen for years,

And to step in all the puddles,

Of all the jealous girls' tears.

You say "Take me as I am",

As if nobody ever does.

But you're the only one who doesn't,

Cause on yourself you only judge.

But if you looked in the mirror,

And just took the time to see,

A beautiful disaster,

You'd never been so pleased.

Acceptance upon yourself,

Because everyone is different,

And if someone's saying you're not the best,

Then you're a damn good competition.

And no matter what, people judge,

Don't let that get you down.

You're a Brasure sister,

We look cute even if we frown,

Appearance, though, is not the point,

You've already got that covered.

A spitting image of your Grams,

Father and your mother.

It's amazing how much I've been through and what I've overcome,

I'm growing up so fast and it scares me but it's fun.

This is my life though and these priorities are my first,

But later on when I go out just somebody hold my purse.

Because I'm young and not in love and not even looking for the one.

Just constantly on the run, but babe I'm just having fun.

So this is the life I live and I'll take it any day,

Because this is the life I was given but I'm happy anyway.

I've never been so curious,
To see how life will be.
To see what comes ahead of us,
For we are only seventeen.
I've never been so wonderous,
To see what comes my way.
To see how I will challenge myself,
Every single day.
I've never been so questionable,
To see the life I'll live.
To see if I will learn to take less,
And in return begin to give.
I've never been so insecure,
About the life I'll lead,
About the difficulties I'll take on,
I just want to see.

I've never been so unhappy,
About the work I've done,
The life I lived before,
Is the past but it's not gone.
I've never been so scared,
To see what life will bring.
To see if I'll have friends,
Or even wear a ring.
I've never cried so hard,
On a dark stormy night,
To see what will happen,
Later on in life.
I've never been so unprepared,
To see what my life will mean.
I've never been so afraid,
For I am only seventeen.

Do you think he knows I'm crying

while we're talking on the phone?

Sitting in this place in which I used to call my home.

Cluttered and a mess – Unorganized stress.

I'm bringing you down

and not giving you my best.

Emptiness swallowed whole in this home I used to know,

With these boxes and these bags,

I'll fucking leave, I said I'd go!

And when you look back and wonder why

and never got to say goodbye

in the right way

just remember,

I actually tried to try.

Whatever happens, happens..
That's all I gotta say.
Cause if I'm headed to tomorrow,
it means I got through today.
No matter where I'm at,
as time passes by,
These days keep coming round,
one more day I didn't die.
Yet with these twists and turns of life,
there are times I don't feel whole.
Tis without these moments I'd lose sanity
and give away my soul.
And in these times of slight confusion
where I'm not sure which way is home.
At least I have my time
It'll always be my own.

I never wanted to be that girl, yet look what I've become.
In shambles all torn up, now look at what you've done.

Let's be done with guys, let's be done with love,

Let's be done with anyone who ever just wanted some.

Let's be done with fears, let's be done with lust,

Let's be done with being too scared of ever wanting to trust.

Let's be done with relationships that only end in hate.

Let's be done with everything that involves us having to wait.

Let's be done with tears, from memories in the past,

Let's be done with hating ourselves because we believed it would last.

Let's be done with lies, let's be done with games,

Let's be done with loving them when all we get is pain.

Let's get over him and let him get over her,

So that then when they come back to us they'll see how real love hurts.

Let's just try for once, not to fall in love,

So that maybe then for once we'll have a little fun.

Let's be done with rules, on this Valentine's,

Today is just for friends who don't want to be with guys.

So raise your lemonade, or whatever you started with,

And remember what real happiness is because this is really it.

Forget the bad, remember the fun, now let's go kick up some dust,

Happy Valentine's Day Brianna, cheers, here's to us!

Stress is the worst.

Because it causes both physical and mental pain.

and the only cure is happiness,

and you can't just buy that at a store.

To all the people that I've hurt and ever put through pain –

To all of those in which I made your tear drops just like rain –

For all the times I've put you down or made you start to frown –

To all of you who cared while I kicked you on the ground –

To the ones in which I gave false hopes and made you wait for texts –

And left you unable to sleep because the thoughts kept you a mess –

To the few of you that fell for me I'm sorry for your pain –

Now I know how you feel as now I feel the same.

Things have been worse, and things will be worse. Things just suck right now. But you will be OK. Because you have been before, and you will be again.

You know that you still love him,

You know that he's the one.

You know how much you miss him,

You know that it's not done.

You know what's on your mind,

You know exactly what you feel,

You know your love is true,

You know that it's for real.

You know that you still want him,

You know that you will try,

You know that you still love him,

With every tear you cry.

He said this is where you belong, lying next to me...

damn near...

no.

right next to me.

He said whenever you come home, babe I may still sleep..

But just know I'm still kissing you even in my dreams.

He said girl you may feel lucky, but I'm in way too deep..

For this love has me mesmerized, I swear I'm counting sheep.

and then he said forever,

and just shimmer looked at me...

if you keep doing what you're doing then babe I'll never leave.

what is it about me

that's got you fallin' hard?

is it my eyes?

or my lips?

what's the very best part?

when I'm near, do you stumble?

if you gave your heart, then would you wonder?

and baby when I'm gone, does your world begin to crumble?

and what's it like going home to that sweet vanilla scent?

better yet just knowing your girls lying in your bed?

so what is it about me?

would you let me see your soul?

and one day will you tell me I'm the one that makes you whole?

You're like a cigarette...

I look forward to you when I'm angry or upset... Stressed.

You put me at ease..

Your taste.

To breathe you in.

I take my time with you.

And after we're done...

it's back to the bullshit.

Yet enough of you could get me high..

I take you in portions to settle my heartbeat.

Damn..

8 months may be another day but I look forward to that cigarette every day.

I wonder if I were an angel,

Sent from god himself.

To only focus on the broken ones,

The souls that needed help.

To help reassure them,

That everything's ok.

All things move forward,

But there will be bad days.

And no matter what my loves,

You are not a mess.

If things were worse just think,

You could have much less.

The flaws and our weaknesses,

The little things we do,

The greatness of our imperfections,

And you let it get to you?

But how could such a beauty,

Such a delicate soul,

Rely on the respect of others,

Just so you'll feel whole?

Alas we must know,

Life is what you make it,

I swear the heavens alone,

Shouldn't be able to take it!

The sacrifices and the struggles,

These feelings we call human,

Everything for tomorrow's chance,

But you don't even want it, do ya?

This bittersweet life,

Where all you get is hurt, and

The only things you don't want

Are the only things to be certain.

Whether it's this life or another.

A different time or place,

I still think I would have helped you,

Without knowing your face.

You are all my angels,

My motivational speech,

I'll always grab your hand

No matter how far you reach.

In sickness and in health,

Till the heavens do part,

We shall walk this together,

Out of the dark.

Sometimes it's harder than you realized, but easier than you expected.

Do you remember birthdays when you were little?

They were so much better than birthdays now.

Nowadays, you go out and party, hang with friends, but barely get anything other than a good time.

You ask for money to pay off your bills or appliances for your new house.

The excitement isn't even there anymore.

Everything in life is so hectic and stressful you forget your birthday is even coming up.

Back then, you'd count down the days until your birthday.

Maybe you even made the loops that you tear off as every day goes by.

A week before your birthday, you make plans to have a birthday party.

With party bags and birthday hats.

You go to the store and order a cake with your name on it and figurines.

You invite all of your friends and family.

Then, when the actual day comes, you're excited to wake up.

You get ready and look your best because it's your special day.

Your friends and family start to show up.

You see the presents arrive and you visually determine what each one will be.

You pick a spot at the dinner table to sit with your closest friends surrounding you.

You see the finished product of a cake come over to the table and sit right in front of you with all the candles lit.

Everyone's taking your picture and you feel like the center of attention.

Everyone sings happy birthday to you but you feel weird just sitting there and it's a little awkward so you dorkishly sing along cause you don't know what else to do.

You open your presents and your eyes light up with everything you unwrap.

Even if you don't like what's inside, you still get excited at just opening up one more gift.

And the presents in the birthday bags are never fun cause you can't unwrap them.

But then the parties over as soon as you cut the cake and eat ice cream.

You have your favorite friends spend the night and the rest leave.

You play with what you got and the next morning it's over.

The only things left are the memories and gifts.

But the day of was the best.

Butterflies, excitement, anxious, everything!

Baby, you are my little kid birthday.

And so when everybody leaves

and you're asked to take a seat,

what do I do when life flashes before me?

Well shit, then I'll just leave.

Go to a different scene..

Do something better

that makes me happy.

And no, you cannot stop me.

Because I'm already gone.

I just keep walking,

to a new kind of home.

If it doesn't matter

then I'll do it alone.

goodnight stress, may we meet again tomorrow.

Today is a new day for me…

and in this day, I will be nothing other than content with everything

and that I am in this new day.

We all have hate within ourselves,
Deep inside beneath the hells,
Raging sounds like righteous bells,

Relieve us from our sins.

With fists and guns we try to solve,
And hatred is a sturdy wall,
Our sanity destroys it all,

No one ever wins.

Corrupted by these violent truths,
Sucking out the useful youths,
Picture perfect cut in two,

How will we survive?

But to stop and say you'd sell your soul,
Feels like quicksand, now your cold,
And after all this hate in bold,

Despicable little lies.

Three pink roses sit on the porches end,

The note sincerely reads: "I'm glad that we're good friends."

Three yellow roses, tied with ribbons, bows, and loops.

The note kindly reads: "I'm very pleased to know you."

Three white roses lay outside my door,

The note sweetly reads: "I'd like to see you more."

Three purple roses, all ends are cut.

The note surprisingly reads: "Let's celebrate us!"

One red rose, handpicked without a root.

The note romantically reads: "I'm falling in love with you."

Three orange roses, so delicate as they lie.

The note swiftly reads: "I just wanted to say hi."

A whole entire garden, planted out by all the trees.

My love cherishingly says: "I just want to make you happy."

Three beautiful roses lie beside my bed.

One yellow, one pink, and of course one is red.

I then look at the note and opened it in two.

And in perfect memory it read: "I remembered and I miss you."

You're like my Edward.

You suck the life right out of me.

But I still sure as hell live for you.

And if it came down to it,

I'd sure as hell die for you.

But no matter what,

You keep going.

And no matter what,

I keep staying.

Trying to protect each other,

By hurting one another,

And even though we know what's right,

You just keep sucking the life right out of me,

And I keep trying to breathe.

What are we supposed to do about this "Love" thing?

Do we let it do the magic for us because we think fate will eventually kick in?

Do we grasp it ourselves and make it happen, even if it takes force?

Do we let it pass by in hopes that something better will come along?

Oh lord, what do we do about this love thing?

Forgive me god for I have sinned

For I have done regretful things.

For I have ate forbidden fruit,

And been greedy from evil's root.

For I have wished what some should not,

And wanted more than what I got.

For I have taken advantage of others,

And have been disrespectful to my father and mother.

For I have hurt the ones I love,

And have a nasty habit of holding a grudge.

For I have hated and wanted death,

Until I realized how much I am blessed.

For I have now seen other's flaws

So I'm asking, please forgive me god.

Please take the bad away from me,

Forgive me god, I'm so sorry.

Give the good to those in need,

And help the ones who cannot read.

Give my hands to the unwritten ones,

For they have better use than what I have done.

Give my eyes to those who don't see,

For I have seen the unbelieved.

Give my tongue to the unspeakable,

For I have said what some shouldn't tell.

Give my ears to those who can't hear,

For I have heard what some do fear.

Give my feet and legs to the unwalkable.

For I have stood and at times fell.

Give my arms to the ones without strength,

For I have pushed and shoved in uncaring ways.

Give my heart to those who can't love,

For it doesn't even matter with what I have done.

And last but not least, make the losers win.

Forgive me god, for I have sinned.

I forgive but don't forget,

I live but don't regret.

I'm stubborn, strong, and know what's wrong,

Because I listened to what Mom said.

And I'll say it without turning red,

Because it's exactly what I meant.

I'll speak the truth and say it with proof,

Even if it doesn't get through your head.

Stupid?

Might as well be dead.

Scared?

Go hide under your bed.

You have to take this life as it comes,

Otherwise you're just used up threads.

it's not that I'm not ready to be someone's princess,
I'm just not ready to have someone be my prince.

Yes I contradict myself

Because I see from both sides.

I get pulled in all directions

and start to lose my mind.

And I'm lucky in knowing

what both sides don't show.

From my experiences I take

the do's and the don'ts.

In this world there are times

when even the confusion has a spell.

Tis in those moments on earth

I see both heaven and hell.

It's been a while since I've baked. I usually do it when I have a lot on my mind. This week I didn't get something that I wanted. I focused my reaction energy into what I do best when no one else is awake. I coded until 4am and accomplished something I didn't think I could on my own just yet.

I made this cake to remind myself that I can do anything. I just have to start and commit to it. This cake took fucking hours. In reality this cake took years of practice, college classes, and shitty cakes that didn't make it.

I always forget how long it actually takes to make a quality cake from scratch.

Focus your energy into what you're passionate about and anything can happen.

Anyone can cook

Anyone can bake.

Anyone can code.

A recipe is an algorithm.

You just have to start.

I didn't put on any makeup today,

It just felt like one of those days.

I knew I was going to cry,

Wearing makeup would've been a waste.

I didn't put on my mascara,

Eyeliner was pointless too.

It would've ended up on my cheeks,

From me crying over you.

All I needed was a tissue,

I didn't need any blush,

There wasn't a use for lip gloss,

I just needed to know there was "us".

I didn't put on any eyeshadow,

What would be the point of that?

All I needed today,

Was to know that you'd come back.

Why try to look pretty?
When all I am is hurt.
What's the point of makeup?
It won't spontaneously make us work.
I'm just gonna roll out of bed,
I won't even do my hair.
I'll just listen to sad songs,
And wish that you were there.
I'm not gonna get dressed up,
I won't even change my clothes,
I'm just gonna lay around,
Because I already know..
I didn't put on any makeup today,
I knew it'd be one of those days,
Just by the way you looked at me,
I knew it'd be one of those days.

This definite possibility;

thoughtless mobility;

driving to my house just so you can kiss me.

and with that being said..

my words turn dead..

the thoughts and the actions..

the readings unread..

the unspoken dares..

in two my heart tears..

run away with me,

        run away with me,

                my love.

Almost 21 years,

that you've put up with me

The struggles and the hug-fulls,

The ponytails and Barbies.

Playing house before your naps,

And business with all my phones.

I never thought I'd see the day,

Where I'd finally have my own.

Nesquik every morning,

With cinnamon or French toast,

It's mornings like that,

Which I'll miss the most.

Jumping up to you,

And wrapping my legs around your waist,

Then you'd just hold me

And put kisses all over my face.

Brina and Caidy you had to deal with too,

Trust me this I know.

But I think I was the hardest,

Because I just didn't want to grow.

I wanted to be your little girl,

For as long as I possibly could be,

But I realize now,

That can still always be me.

A mother's job is difficult,
But you did it so well.
For now I'm all grown up,
With stories of you to tell.
I am now a woman,
You did this to me.
Not so little anymore,
But with who you made me I am pleased.
I would have chosen you as my mother,
If you weren't given to me at birth.
And anytime we have differences,
I'm sorry, for what it's worth.
Anything I say,
Could never be enough,
For everything you've done for me.
I thank you so much.
I love you more than anything,
You raised us all so well.
You deserve this day,
And we'll still call you for help.
We can do things on our own now,
I'll have kids one day too,
And when I become a mother,
I would have learned everything from you.

Think of it like this, words were created long ago and developed to rhyme with other words, so I could put them in a fluent poem to give to you.

Yes, that's how and why words were created, so I could tell you one day I love you.

Words match up for us, just as you match up for me.

I'd just like for the unimaginable to be imagined and the impossible to be possible.

Because these days are like vinegar in water and I can't keep trying to make things come together.

You're not the deciding factor,

You're not even what really matters.

I've done this before in the past and even then I was better after.

You're not what makes this whole,

This time I have control.

Thanks for the recognition, but it's still not your fucking decision!

I'm seriously done with the chasing.

The circles of racing and pacing.

Finding out I can do better, get back the time that I've been wasting.

According to a daisy...he *loves* me.

But I swear to god I love every second

and I promise myself I'll never regret it!

Within myself I knew I deserved it; this happiness when you feel life's perfect.

And no one person can hurt me now,

only I have the power to break me down!

But don't act like I have careless ways..this is my life, I pick who stays.

My head, my heart, my body, and soul,

maintaining my happiness, maintaining control.

I don't think it matters what a person looks like for you to care for them. Not even some personality traits matter after a certain point. You learn to accept that person for who they are whether they fit your type before or not. Everything you wanted goes out the window because you have developed a sudden interest at heart for this individual. And now, those are the things you look for in someone. Your heart has persuaded you once again.

I have this vision...we're driving...and we crash...and I'm finally truly happy again.

Why??

Because he loves my stupid hair and these dull green eyes.

Kisses me just once and I'm instantly hypnotized.

Texts me in the morning just to make me smile.

Then comes to my door and surprises me with flowers.

And for some reason he likes my laugh, and I can't help but wonder why.

I feel like I could trust him, like he'd never lie.

And I know he gets those tingles, yea those butterflies.

May cover it up well but he's shakin deep inside.

Dear great one, oh great one,
I must thank you,
For all of the things,
I know that you do.
Great one, oh great one,
Who or whatever you may be,
I appreciate everything
In which you've provided for me.
Great one, yes great one,
For I know it is you,
The reason I'm here,
And able to move.
The reason for all
of the decisions I make.
For every lesson I've learned,
Excuses for every mistake.
The power behind me,
Allowing me to breathe,
Offering me to stay,
Even when I want to leave.
Great one, but great one,
How could this be?
When I haven't even met you,
Yet you've done all this for me?
Great one, oh great one,
Do you even exist?

For it seems like most people,

May need you to assist.

But I know you are busy,

And are doing your best,

But you helped me!

And for that I am blessed.

You may not know this,

But I'm sure you do.

You've saved me once or twice,

And others I love, too.

Great one, oh great one,

I don't know who you are.

But you've taken me down a road,

And I've made it this far.

And it isn't just about me,

Great damn it! I swear.

Because they told me when they needed you

That you were right there.

Great one, oh great one,

Words couldn't express,

The affection I have

For life's effects.

Someone or something,

I know nothing about,

Yet I feel you are there,

In some form or cloud.

Great one, oh great one,

Is this heaven on earth?

Or is it hell on the universe?

Some days I'm not sure.

There has to be something up there,

It's still hard for me to believe,

And selfish of myself,

To only see when goods are received.

Oh great one, dear great one,

And I'll thank you one day in spirit,

For all of the accomplishments you allowed me to have,

And giving me the strength to not fear it.

How come as soon as I seem to get over the heartbreak you've caused me you come back just to sweep me off my feet again. Is it that you like seeing me hurt? Am I not allowed to move on and be happy? Why do you keep coming back just to leave again?

I've never had time go by so fast, it's almost as if I'm losing life instead of gaining it. Maybe I'm spending my time the wrong way, or maybe time is just spending me.

where does the time go?

into a lupe hole?

    or loop hole and

        repeat

        repeat itself?

        where has the time gone for I cannot find you.

They're fighting over there,

They're fighting for their lives.

They're fighting for their rights,

Their children and their wives.

They're struggling over there,

They're struggling till it gives.

They're struggling so much

Until there's nothing left to struggle with.

They're screaming over there,

They're screaming their lungs out.

They're screaming till they lose their voice,

They're screaming right out loud.

They're killing over there,

They're killing cause they're forced.

They're killing and they're killing

And now they have remorse.

They're crying over there,

They're shedding many tears,

They're crying over there

Because they're faced with all their fears.

They're praying over there,

They're praying for their strength.

They're praying for this war

To have a shorter length.

They're begging over there,

They're begging for a chance.

They're begging to go home alive

And hold their wives' hands.

They're dying over there,

They're dying all for us.

They're dying so that we don't have to,

And because they simply feel they must.

It's like should I jump?

Would it matter?

What would happen???

That's a lota cigarettes man.

It's like tight, thorn vines
Securely wrapped around my wrists.
Cutting off my circulation when
I clench and raise my fists.
Although it hurts more,
I somehow have to fight,
Or I'd be tangled forever,
Wrapped in pain so tight.
And yet I let it burn,
And my wounds begin to seep.
I'm wide awake in torture,
But you're not losing any sleep.
I'm tangled babe, I'm tangled.
Such unbearable pain,
It only hurts worse,
When I try to break away.

I'm tangled babe, I'm tangled.

But the worst is yet to come,

For when I am free,

To you I'll start to run.

Knowing one day,

I'll be tangled once again.

With these thorns and these vines,

I'll be happy when it ends.

I'm tangled babe, I'm tangled.

And all you do is watch.

The attention is what I thrive on,

And the yield comes to a stop.

Babe, you know I'm strangled,

Slowly suffocating me,

To breathe one more time,

But only if I'm free.

I had a dream last night that I was going into the army.

I was all suited up, had all that I needed with me..

I'd be gone for a while..

and as we started to drive off, I heard explosions..

I had been trained for this..

I don't even think I was scared..

and all that was on my mind was you....

How do you unravel

from such twisted desires?

When you're used to walking

through a million wildfires?

And the pokes and the pins

that pierce from deep within...

How do I,

How do I..

    Unravel from this?

100 years I give to you,

It could be more, it could be less.

Depending on your health issues,

And how you handle stress.

Will you love or will you hate?

Will you give or will you take?

Will you dwell upon your past?

Or future memories to make?

100 years is all you get,

Every day deserves a tally.

And remember to always be cautious,

Because luck isn't down every alley.

Will you stay or will you go?

Will you let your knowledge grow?

And if there's something on your mind,

Will you let those people know?

87 years.

All from broken hearts.

It really takes a toll,

On all those tally marks.

Will you wish or will you pray?

Or will you work it day by day?

What is it that you will do,

To get out of all that grey?

64 years

And we have all these bills.

The side effects of life,

Some people steal, hurt, and kill.

But why is it this way?

To learn, we make mistakes.

And you can't tell me if I wanted to save you

That I'd be a second late.

52 years.

And it was all for what?

To stress myself out

Over meaningless stuff.

Take these moments and you cherish them.

Never let your worries perish friends.

And if there's someone that you're fighting with,

Just try to make amends.

Because 47 it comes so fast
And you look at what you've done.
Work, cried, and broken hearts,
But where was all the fun?
Experience the best.
Say fuck it to the rest.
And whatever you're holding back,
Just get it off your chest.
The years that we shave off
Could have been smiles added on.
It depends on how you live your life,
And what you think you're doing wrong.
Take life within your hands,
Fuck all those other demands.
Just do whatever it is you want,
Don't worry about making plans.
Just take everything as it comes,
And make everything a memory,
And when you find yourself blaming life,
Remember we are our own worst enemy.

It's silly to avoid life.

I wanna love you a bunch,

    love you too much,

    give you the world,

but that's still not enough.

    Breathe in your soul,

    and exhale the toll,

    of what I would pay

for you making me whole.

    Show you a life,

with me doing you right,

    one hundred percent,

I don't have to think twice.

    No matter the days,

    it's my heart that stays,

and I'll keep loving you,

    in 900 billion ways..

(even china)

the difference between 'but' & 'and'....

I love you,
but I'm not in love with you.

I'm overwhelmed with you,
but in a good way.

I'm crazy about you,
and it won't stop.

you're everything I've ever wanted
and so much more.

I may leave you in the day,
but I'll always come back.

I remember the days when I had things to do...

...fun things.

Getting ready was something to look forward to.

Haven't taken my bathrobe off

                now

                      for quite

                        some

                            time.

Maybe I'm supposed to be confused, in this spot right now.

I know I can change it I'm just not sure which way to put the sail.

Who knows what or where I'm supposed to be right now.

Where I am isn't so bad right now.

But it can always be better.

So it scares me when I think, "if I took a huge leap, maybe I could be that much more awesome."

To save someone, to help myself, be in a right-place-right-time situation.

I'm never in any situation. I'm just me.

So wherever and whenever life takes me, I know I'll be ready.

I just hope it doesn't hurt the people around me anymore.

Because I just want the world to be happy.

If I were a bird, who knows where I'd be.

I don't know where I'm supposed to be right now.

Where am I going?

What am I doing?

Who am I supposed to be?

My life isn't that bad.

I have an amazing boyfriend who I couldn't tell you how amazing he is.

I have a great family that's pretty close considering how far we've grown apart.

And I'm not completely broke.

There's always more I'll want, more I'll want to do.

But right now I'd say I'm pretty content.

So why am I so sad all the time?

I get so angry, but why?

People look at me and think maybe I have some flaws and maybe my life isn't perfect, but how bad could that girl's life really be?

It's not that bad!

But I'm always so sad and angry and I take it out on everyone I love when really I just want to beat myself up.

Do I really want to help people with themselves if I can't even help myself with me?!

Who am I?

Where am I going?

What am I doing?

And why for the life of me can I not figure it out?

Because he loves me with no make up on and a pair of baggy sweats.

My hair straight down, and a hint of vanilla scent.

Then he kisses me on my forehead and makes my heart beat fast.

Does everything for me and I don't even have to ask.

And when we go to bed he says I love you with his eyes.

Just a few reasons why we fall for guys.

and as I laid on my bedroom floor in complete sadness I realized I really need to vacuum.

I didn't know you very well, and I didn't need to. We weren't sisters, or best friends. We were acquaintances in passing connected by mutual bonds but I still would have been there to try and save you. We didn't have to be best friends. We just had to be humans. Simple. Simple fucking humans in such an intricate, fucked up world. To know it got the best of someone, the amount of rage it brings. We all would have liked for you to stay. But that feeling of urgency to leave.. I hope I never made you feel alone. I am so sorry for the battles you have fought for however long ago they started, but today the world has it's own battle to face in losing such a gem.

Today you are happy.

Today you are free.

May you be in peace for eternity

Dear Doug,

I found out today you are gone.

And that you have been for a little while now.

But I will never forget helping you finish your broccoli so you could move onto something else. Or doing your potato skins for you so you could get out a little early. I will never forget the French CD that you gave me and Mandy. Or your surprised look when I said something inappropriate. I'll never forget giving you your melted butter. Or you letting me use your good knife. Or talking to you about life. Looking back, I'm glad I helped you with even the small things, knowing you might have gotten out of work a little earlier to enjoy your days...or even make your work days better. You were the nicest, sweetest man, with the kindest heart. That smile will not be forgotten.

Enjoy your stay in paradise ♥

Life is too short to live by the rules. And it's certainly too short to love by the rules. In fight or flight I will always choose flight, because I refuse to stay on the ground forever and nobody can tell me I can't fly. I will choose the closest thing to airborne freedom and I will jump out of a plane again. Life is too short, and sometimes love is too, to not think outside of the box and to not do things that make you feel lifted. When you have these feelings, you must do whatever it is you're feeling, it is a gift to yourself. And honestly, you owe it to yourself to experience that in this life. Whatever it is, just do it. Because there is absolutely no reason not to.

And if you ever think of taking your own life, remember the second after you do you'll be on the other side screaming no.

Life is too short, for anything and everything. Be free. Be peaceful. Be anything that makes you happy. And do anything that makes you feel alive. Don't worry about the time, it's already passing anyway. Just live it. Nobody ever had a good time staring at their watch. Be extravagant. Be optimistic. More importantly, be realistic. Never expect anything and just try to give. Care more. Judge less. And know the meaningful things are awaiting you. Be outgoing. Be fucking adventurous. Be free.

…and I'm letting him take me on a date because I'm sick of wondering what would happen.

he reminds me of you... but better.
so i did the same things to him... but worse.
and he understood... like you didn't.
but he tells me things... and i smile.
i don't worry... because i trust him.
yet i'm scared... because he's a better you.
so i wonder... if it'll be more painful.
then i think... he's not you at all.
and then... i smile again.

home.

where I can finally sleep after this shitday at work.

home.

where I can walk in and feel relieved immediately.

home.

where I can walk around in the dark and still know where not to bump in to.

home.

where I can play and be as loud as I want.

home.

where everyone is welcome to be at ease.

home.

where I can do whatever I want in any room I choose.

home.

where comfortability is encouraged.

home.

where I know food will be made properly and taste amazing.

home.
where it smells like vanilla and chaos.

home.
where I can say whatever the fuck I want.

home.
where porn is accepted in places other than the bathroom.

home.
where failure is never frowned upon.

home.
where I can take my time.

home.
where I can breathe.

home.
where i can just.. be.

yeah,
there's no place like home.

A Day of No Worry

I would wake up rested. And smile. In no rush for anything other than my beautiful life. I wouldn't need coffee, for I would already be energized from within. I would radiate peace and fearlessness. Because on a day with no worries, there is nothing to fear. I would roll out of bed, which was more comfortable than any other time due to my peace of mind, and I would prance around as if I had things to look forward to. But those things would be nothingness, and it would be the best damn feeling I had ever had. The sun would be shining and I would be smiling and there would be nothing at that particular moment that I would rather be doing. And maybe for a moment I would sit. And ponder about all of the worries in which I didn't have. I would appreciate all of the times I felt stress and be grateful that on this day, this day of no worries whatsoever, I can think of other things. The more important things. Everything that truly matters rolled up into one "I can finally put you in front of my mind" ball. I wouldn't have to think about the bills, the laundry, the traffic, the long line at the nearest grocery store. I wouldn't need to worry about the pleasing of others, unless I wanted to. It would all be about peace. And on this day of no worries, it wouldn't just be me who had no worries, no. It would be everyone. My neighbors, my family, coworkers, strangers. The world. A day of no worries. A day of peace. Could you imagine? The whole world having nothing to stress about, nothing to displease them, nothing to put pressure on them, nothing to make them feel as if they are pressed for time to do something or get something done that probably doesn't even really matter as much as they were told it was. No fighting, nor struggling, nor pushing, nor shoving. There would be no hurting, or breaking, or taking, none of it. For one day we would all be....just, be. We could sit there in silence and know we were just feeling each other's energy and vibrations. All of our currents as one only because we were focused on the positivity of this one day that we have been granted. For once we are all free in spirit and able to strive in such a different manner than ever before. If you fall I will catch you, and you would do the same for me. There would be no "bothering"....we could all relax. And with one another on our no worry day, we would focus so much on everything there is that is good and focus so much on the great things we all have and the things we feel we no longer need due to our new found clarifications. This day would be a day of findings. And we would all be in exceptional bliss. Humans being nice to other humans. But not just nice; courteous, considerate, we would all be in understanding with each other of this day and what it meant and what it was worth to one another. We would all be friends, we would all be a family. Connected through our energies. This day would be stimulating. We would mentally be healthier. Making us all feel better inside and out. Overall, this day would be the first to which we didn't shave time off of our lives, simply because we were not obligated to do anything we did not feel necessary. In a sense, for that day...we would find peace. In ourselves. In one another. In this crazy, chaotic world. In this mess we live in we would find pure peace on this one no worry day. And in these moments we would find a way to make that one day last. And you cannot tell me for a single damn minute that the next day you would be able to just wake up and go back to the way things used to be. No, not after a day like that.

3/21/2015

(A blog post for a previous blog I started and ultimately closed because I wasn't consistent and didn't entirely believe in myself – It was called lannabehappy)

Thank you for taking a peek inside of my soul

I hope you resonated with something.

You will be ok.

♥

www.ingramcontent.com/pod-product-compliance
Lightning Source LLC
Chambersburg PA
CBHW071118160426
43196CB00013B/2616